WACKY WORDS

WACKY
WORDS

WORLD BOOK, INC.
CHICAGO LONDON SYDNEY TORONTO

World Book, Inc.
525 W. Monroe
Chicago, IL 60661
U.S.A.

ISBN: 0-7166-4103-8

LC: 96-60276

Cover design: Design 5

For information on other World Book products, call 1-800-255-1750, X2238,
or visit us at our Web site at http://www.worldbook.com

Printed in Singapore

2 3 4 5 99 98

Introduction

Puzzles are fun. They challenge our imagination and make us think. But they are also a way of learning *how* to think. And they can also help us to learn things without even realizing it.

The puzzles in this book are *word* puzzles. They ask you to find hidden words, make words from pictures, take words apart and rearrange them, and so on. You'll need a pencil and paper so that you can write things down.

To solve these puzzles, it helps if you know lots of words and their meanings. If you do a lot of reading, these puzzles should be easy—and lots of fun. Don't be disappointed if you can't solve a puzzle. Read the answer carefully to see how it was worked out. Then you'll find that the next puzzle may be a little easier to solve.

Rhyming pairs

On this page, there are five pairs of things whose names rhyme. Can you pick out each pair?

(ANSWERS ON PAGE 30)

Rebus

A rebus is a puzzle in which pictures, letters, and numbers stand for words. In some cases, you must subtract a letter from a word, or from the name of an object, to get the right word. This rebus contains three words that mean a lot to everyone.

(ANSWER ON PAGE 30)

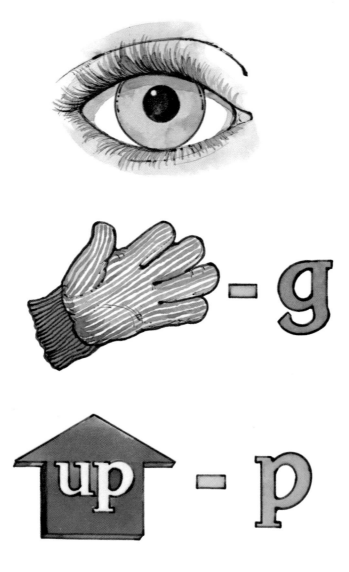

Beheaded words

To behead a word, you chop off the first letter. Sometimes, when you do this, you get a brand-new word.

Here's a puzzle that gives you clues to words that change into other words when they're beheaded. For example, behead the word that means the opposite of closed, and you'll get the word that means a place where pigs are kept, or a tool to write with. The word is *open*. When you behead it, you get *pen*.

Ready? Go.

1. Behead the word that means "not fast," and you'll get the word that means "not high."

2. Behead the word that means "a sandy place by water" and you'll get the word that means "every single one."

3. Behead the word that's the name of a black bird and you'll get the word for what you do to make a small boat move.

4. Behead the word for what you think with and you'll get the word for falling water.

5. Behead the word for a scare and you'll get the word that's the opposite of wrong.

6. Behead the word that means "tidy" and you'll get the word for what you want to do at lunchtime.

Here are some harder beheading puzzles.

7. Behead the word that means "hard work" and you'll get the word for something cars need.

8. Behead the word for a precious metal and you'll get the word for something that has been around a long time.

9. Behead the word for a tool that helps you reach a high place and you'll get the name of a poisonous snake.

10. Behead the word for a tool that's used to smooth wood and you'll get the word for a small road.

11. Behead the word that means "to make a hole" and you'll get the word for the material that metal comes from.

12. Behead the word that means "sleep" and you'll get the word that means "wood for building."

(ANSWERS ON PAGE 30)

Turnaround words

When you spell most words backwards, you get a word that doesn't mean anything, such as girl—lrig. But sometimes when you turn a word around you get a new, real word. For example, spell *rat* backwards and you get *tar*.

Here are clues to some words that become new words when they're turned around. See how many you can get.

1. Turn around a word for a number and get a word for something with which you catch fish.

2. Turn around a word for a tool to cook with and get a word for something a baby often does.

3. Turn around a word that means "at this very moment" and get a word for something that is gained by a victory.

4. Turn around the word for a thing you do work with and get the word for something pirates were always seeking.

5. Turn around a word that means "not dead," and get a word that means "very, very bad."

6. Turn around a word for someone who isn't truthful and you'll get a word for something a train needs.

(ANSWERS ON PAGE 30)

Opposites

What's the opposite of *cold*? *Hot*, of course.
See if you can think of the opposite for each
of these words. Each opposite is *one* word.

1. more

2. new

3. first

4. ahead

5. wet

6. high

7. far

8. early

Here are some more words for which to find opposites. *But*, each opposite must be a word that begins with the letter *s*.

1. crooked   5. dangerous

2. happy   6. weak

3. dull   7. calm

4. hard   8. quick

(ANSWERS ON PAGE 30)

Changeover

Changeover is a game in which you change a word, one letter at a time, until you have a word that means the opposite of the word you started with. However, each time you change a letter, you must have a *real* word. Here's how to change **some** to **none** in three moves.

1. Change **some** to **come** by changing **s** to **c**.

2. Change **come** to **cone** by changing **m** to **n**.

3. Change **cone** to **none** by changing **c** to **n**.

And so, you've gone from some to none— a complete changeover! Now, try these changeovers on your own.

1. Change **glee** to **glum** in two moves.

2. Change **hill** to **vale** in three moves.

3. Change **more** to **less** in four moves.

4. Change **cold** to **heat** in four moves.

5. Change **hard** to **soft** in six moves.

(ANSWERS ON PAGE 30)

Strange lands

Five children who were traveling with their parents met at an airport. Although they all came from different countries, they found they all spoke the same language. But, just for fun, each child scrambled up the name of his or her country so the others would have to figure out what the real name was.

- Joe said he was from Andaca.

- Gail came from Duneti Testas.

- Molly was from Clonstad.

- Juanita came from an island called Turpeo Crio.

- Peter proudly stated he was from Tiasalura.

By rearranging the letters of each name, you can find out where each child was really from.

(ANSWERS ON PAGE 30)

A test for poets

Are you a poet—and don't know it? To find
out, see if you can fill in the right word in the
blank space in each of these little poems. But
remember, the words must not only rhyme, they
must also make sense.

1. I eat my peas with honey.
   I've done it all my life.
   It makes the peas taste funny,
   but they can't slide off my _____.

2. There was an old man from Peru,
   Who dreamed he was eating his shoe.
   He awoke in a fright,
   In the middle of the night,
   And found it was perfectly _____.

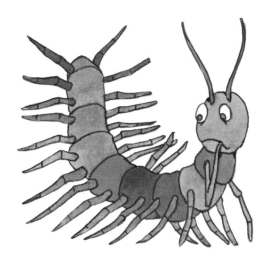

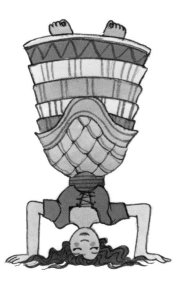

3. A centipede with thirty feet
   To himself said, "I refuse
   To spend the money I know it will take
   To buy myself new _____."

4. There was a young lady of Crete
   Who was most exceedingly neat.
   When she got out of bed,
   She stood on her head,
   To make sure of not soiling her _____.

(ANSWERS ON PAGE 30)

Put-together words

A lot of words are made out of sounds that are actually *other* words—short words that usually have nothing to do with the word they help to make. For example, *car*, a vehicle, and *pet*, a tame, owned animal, form the word *carpet*, a floor covering.

Here are clues for pairs of short words that can be put together to form other words. All the short words are words you know, although some of the words they make may be new to you.

1. Put together a word that's the name of part of your head and a word that means "a baby bird's home." You'll get a word that means "firm and serious."

2. Put together a word that's the name for part of a book and a word that's the name of an insect. You'll have a word that means "a showy spectacle or parade."

3. Put together a word that means "a small bed" and a word that's the name of a measure of weight. You'll have the name of a kind of cloth.

4. Put together a word that's the name of a cooking tool and a word that means "an attempt." You'll have the name of a small room where food is kept.

5. Put together a word that's the name of a head covering and a word that means the amount of space a thing takes up. You'll have a word that means "to overturn."

(ANSWERS ON PAGE 31)

Hidden words

Hidden in the next sentence is the name of a piece of furniture.

March air is often quite chilly.

Did you find it? The word is *chair.* It's made up of the *ch* in Mar*ch* followed by the word *air.*

In each of the sentences below is hidden the name of a thing you would probably want to take along on a picnic. Each thing is something to eat.

1. You can pick less fruit by hand than you can with a machine.

2. "There are two cats up in a tree," cried Jan.

3. Frank sings alto in the church choir.

4. Ants cannot eat wood, but termites can.

5. The college will enroll students in the fall.

(ANSWERS ON PAGE 31)

Rearranged words

In each of the sentences below there is one word that can be changed into a different word by rearranging the letters. Each sentence makes sense as it now is. But, if you can find the right word to change, the sentence will take on a new meaning.

For example: "We'll have to walk around this little loop of water," said Bob. The word that can be changed is *loop*. Perhaps there *could* be a *loop* of water formed by a tiny stream, so the sentence makes sense. But, when you change *loop* to *pool*, the sentence becomes more meaningful.

1. "I got a sore from that thorny bush," announced Mary.

2. "I have to put my hoses in the closet," called Jerry.

3. If you prod a drinking glass, it will probably break.

4. "Hear that low hooting in the woods?" asked Brian.

5. Church bells often seem to sound as if they're leaping for joy.

6. A fox crouched beside a rail in the forest.

7. "I saw a reed beside the river," said Jane.

(ANSWERS ON PAGE 31)

21

The Ongloti language

Can you read Ongloti? You can if you are reading this!

English is full of different letter combinations with the same sounds. The *o* in *women* sounds like the *i* in *win*. And the *ti* in *station* sounds like the *sh* in *shadow*. So, if you spell *English* with the *o* from *women* for the two *i* sounds and the *ti* from *station* for the *sh* sound, you get *Ongloti*!

Here are some other letter combinations and their sounds: the *ei* in *neighbor* sounds like the *a* in *nay*; the *o* in *one* sounds like the *w* in *won*; the *gh* in *tough* sounds like the *f* in *muff*, and the *or* in *work* sounds like the *ir* in *sir*. Keeping these in mind, can you figure out the following Ongloti words? There is a hint with each one.

1. oond   It can move things.

2. tielgh   You put things on it.

3. gheid   This often happens to clothes.

4. ghorst   It's number one.

(ANSWERS ON PAGE 31)

The two scientists

A scientist was looking through a telescope. Suddenly she turned to another scientist who stood nearby and exclaimed, "No more stars!"

What kind of scientists were they? You can find out by rearranging the letters in the words the scientists said.

(ANSWERS ON PAGE 31)

What's for breakfast?

In the country of Injuh, a man walked into a restaurant and sat down at a table. A waitress came over to him.

"FUNEM?" asked the man.

"SVFM," replied the waitress.

"FUNEX?" asked the man.

"SVFX," said the waitress.

"OK," said the man. "LFMNX."

Do you know what they said to each other?

(ANSWERS ON PAGE 32)

The pup's tale

A number of words in English read the same backwards as forwards. Such a word, for example, is *toot*. Another is *bib*, the cloth a baby wears under its chin when it eats.

A word that reads the same backwards or forwards is called a **palindrome** (PAL ihn drohm). See how many palindromes you can find in the following story:

The police had been called. The Smiths' family pet, a collie pup, had been stolen!

"Sis took him for a walk, at noon," said Mom, pointing to her little girl. "She stopped to buy a bottle of pop. When she turned around, the dog was gone."

The little girl was crying bitterly. Tears poured from each eye, and her face was redder than a radish.

"I wonder who did such a deed?" muttered the policeman. "I'll level with you; only a real dud would steal from such a tiny tot!"

"Wow!" Dad suddenly cried. "Look!"

There in the yard was the dog. It hadn't been stolen at all, just lost. And it had found its way home like an airplane following a radar signal!

(ANSWERS ON PAGE 32)

What's in a name?

There are often hidden words in people's names. Here are some riddles about names with hidden words in them. Each riddle asks a question about the person, and the answer is always, "Because there's a, or an (the hidden word), in his name." For example, a riddle about the name EARL might be: "Why can EARL hear so well?" Answer— "Because there's an EAR in his name (EARL)." See how it works?

1. Why is JANICE always cold?

2. Why is MILTON so heavy?

3. Why is JOYCE always happy?

4. Why can MARTIN draw so well?

5. Why can't you believe LESLIE?

6. Why doesn't CHRISTOPHER ever finish things?

7. Why doesn't RACHEL feel well?

8. Why can't you trust PATRICK?

9. Why can JANET catch fish so easily?

10. Why should EDWARD be a soldier?

11. Why does CHARLOTTE have so much of everything?

12. Why does STEWART always have plenty to eat?

(ANSWERS ON PAGE 32)

Animal, vegetable, mineral

Have you ever played the game called "Animal, Vegetable, or Mineral"? One person thinks of something that's animal, vegetable, or mineral. Then another person tries to find what it is by asking twenty questions.

Here's a different kind of animal, vegetable, mineral game. It is made up of twelve scrambled words. Four words are the names of things that belong to the animal kingdom, four belong to the vegetable kingdom, and four belong to the mineral kingdom. (Minerals are the lifeless things that come out of the earth, such as metals, rocks, and jewels.) The names aren't in any order. There's a clue with each, to help you figure out what it is. But—the clues are tricky!

1. NOFWESRUL
   It likes sunshine.

2. DALREEM
   It's bright green.

3. YISAD
   It lives in meadows.

4. BLUEBEMEB
   You may find one in your backyard.

5. OPREDLA
   It's orange and black.

6. TAINREG

You see it on many buildings.

7. DODMINA

Some people say it's their best friend.

8. HYNTOP

It might squeeze you very tight.

9. PEALP

It's hard and red.

10. LUTTER

It has a hard shell.

11. PROCEP

It's shiny orange at first, but turns brown
or green as it gets old.

12. BERBRU

Cars roll down the road on it.

(ANSWERS ON PAGE 32)

Answers

Rhyming pairs (PAGE 6)

1—E: goat—boat
2—D: book—cook
3—A: fish—dish
4—B: tree—key
5—C: mouse—house

Rebus (PAGE 7)

I love you

Beheaded words (PAGE 8)

1. slow; low
2. beach; each
3. crow; row
4. brain; rain
5. fright; right
6. neat; eat

More beheadings

7. toil; oil
8. gold; old
9. ladder; adder
10. plane; lane
11. bore; ore
12. slumber; lumber

Turnaround words (PAGE 10)

1. ten—net
2. pan—nap
3. now—won
4. tool—loot
5. live—evil
6. liar—rail

Opposites (PAGE 12)

1. more—less
2. new—old
3. first—last
4. ahead—behind
5. wet—dry
6. high—low
7. far—near
8. early—late

Opposites beginning with s

1. crooked—straight
2. happy—sad
3. dull—sharp
4. hard—soft
5. dangerous—safe
6. weak—strong
7. calm—stormy
8. quick—slow

Changeover (PAGE 14)

1. Change **glee** to **glue** and **glue** to **glum**.
2. Change **hill** to **hall**; **hall** to **hale** (which means healthy); and **hale** to **vale** (a small valley).
3. Change **more** to **lore** (stories about a certain subject); **lore** to **lose**; **lose** to **loss**; and **loss** to **less**.
4. Change **cold** to **hold**; **hold** to **held**; **held** to **head**; and **head** to **heat**.
5. Change **hard** to **card**; **card** to **cart**; **cart** to **part**; **part** to **port**; **port** to **sort**; and **sort** to **soft**.

Strange lands (PAGE 15)

Andaca is Canada.
Duneti Testas is the United States.
Clonstad is Scotland.
Turpeo Crio is Puerto Rico.
Tiasalura is Australia.

A test for poets (PAGE 16)

1. knife—to rhyme with life
2. true—to rhyme with shoe
3. shoes—to rhyme with refuse
4. feet—to rhyme with neat

Answers

Put-together words (PAGE 18)

1. ear + nest = earnest—firm and serious
2. page + ant = pageant—a showy spectacle
3. cot + ton = cotton—a kind of cloth
4. pan + try = pantry—a small room
5. cap + size = capsize—overturn

Hidden words (PAGE 20)

1. Pickles. You will *pick les*s fruit by hand than you can with a machine.
2. Catsup. "There are two *cats up* in a tree," cried Jan.
3. Salt. Frank sings *alt*o in the church choir.
4. Butter. Ants cannot eat wood, *but ter*mites can.
5. Rolls. The college will en*roll* students in the fall.

Rearranged words (PAGE 21)

1. sore—rose You probably could get a *sore* from a thorny bush if you pricked yourself on a thorn. But what Mary really got from the thorny bush was a *rose*.
2. hoses—shoes Some people might keep *hoses* in a closet, but what Jerry was putting there was his *shoes*.

3. prod—drop A *prod*, or push, probably wouldn't cause a glass to break, but if you *drop* it, it would surely shatter.
4. low—owl If you were to hear *low* hooting in a woods, it would probably be an *owl* doing the hooting.
5. leaping—pealing Church bells may seem to sound as if they're *leaping* for joy. But we call the sound that church bells make *pealing*.
6. rail—lair There might well be a *rail* in a forest, but a fox would be more likely to crouch beside a *lair*, which is the name for an animal's hiding place.
7. reed—deer A *reed* could grow beside a river, but reeds grow in big clusters, not just one. What Jane saw was a *deer*.

The Ongloti language
(PAGE 22)

1. oond—wind: The *w* sound is the *o* from *one* and the *i* sound is the *o* from *women*.
2. tielgh—shelf: The *sh* sound is the *ti* from *station* and the *f* sound is the *gh* from *tough*.
3. gheid—fade: The *f* sound is the *gh* from *tough* and the *a* sound is the *ei* from *neighbor*.
4. ghorst—first: The *f* sound is the *gh* from *tough* and the *ur* sound is the *or* from *work*.

The two scientists (PAGE 23)

The letters in "No more stars" can be arranged to make the word *astronomers*. Astronomers are scientists who study the stars.

Answers

What's for breakfast? (PAGE 24)

You can tell what the man and the waitress said to each other if you say each letter aloud *as a letter*.

The man says F-U-N-E-M. Say each letter aloud and you'll see that it sounds as if the man were saying "Have you any ham?"

The waitress says S-V-F-M, or "Yes, we have ham."

The man says F-U-N-E-X, or "Have you any eggs?"

S-V-F-X, says the waitress, or "Yes, we have eggs."

So, the man says, O-K. L-F-M-N-X, or "Okay. I'll have ham and eggs."

The pup's tale (PAGE 25)

There are fifteen different palindromes in the story. In the order in which they appear, they are:

pup	mom	redder	level	wow
sis	pop	did	dud	dad
noon	eye	deed	tot	radar

What's in a name? (PAGE 26)

1. Because there's ICE in her name (JAN**ICE**)
2. Because there's a TON in his name (MIL**TON**)
3. Because there's JOY in her name (**JOY**CE)
4. Because there's ART in his name (M**ART**IN)
5. Because there's a LIE in her name (LES**LIE**)
6. Because there's a STOP in his name (CHRI**STOP**HER)
7. Because there's an ACHE in her name (R**ACHE**L)
8. Because there's a TRICK in his name (PA**TRICK**)
9. Because there's a NET in her name (JA**NET**)
10. Because there's WAR in his name (ED**WAR**D)
11. Because there's a LOT in her name (CHAR**LOT**TE)
12. Because there's STEW in his name (**STEW**ART)

Animal, vegetable, mineral (PAGE 28)

1. NOFWESRUL—SUNFLOWER (vegetable)
2. DALREEM—EMERALD (mineral)
3. YISAD—DAISY (vegetable)
4. BLUEBEMEB—BUMBLEBEE (animal)
5. OPREDLA—LEOPARD (animal)
6. TAINREG—GRANITE (mineral)
7. DODMINA—DIAMOND (mineral)
8. HYNTOP—PYTHON (animal)
9. PEALP—APPLE (vegetable)
10. LUTTER—TURTLE (animal)
11. PROCEP—COPPER (mineral)
12. BERBRU—RUBBER (vegetable)